Drawn to the Heavens

My Story of Love, Devotion, and Perseverance in the Face of Adversity

Drawn to the Heavens

My Story of Love, Devotion, and Perseverance in the Face of Adversity

By Robert J. Atkins

DRAWN TO THE HEAVENS: MY STORY OF LOVE, DEVOTION, AND PERSEVERANCE IN THE FACE OF ADVERSITY

Independently published in the United States of America. Copyright © 2019 by Robert J. Atkins

All rights reserved. No part of this publication may be reproduced, distributed, or transmitted in any form or by any means, including photocopying, recording, or electronic or mechanical methods, without the prior written permission of the author or publisher.

ISBN: 978-1-7341240-0-2

Contact Bob Atkins: bobajump1@gmail.com

Edited by Stephanie J. Beavers Communications
www.StephanieJBeavers.com / 610–247–9494

Photo of Virginia Tech Tribute Skydive taken by Selena Marks. Photo appeared in the June 2007 issue of the USPA Parachutist magazine.

Cover by Biddle Design / www.biddledesign.com

Cover photo taken at the North Pole by a fellow traveler and skydiver.

Dedication

For Jane, who accepts me as I am.

In Memory Of

Earl "Rocky" Radabaugh

John "Jay" Frantz

"Handsome Dave" DeWolf

Contents

Introduction xi
The Jobs I Loved 1
Life Was Good 7
The Accident 9
The Stroke 15
The Seizure 23
Sis's Dream Trip 25
Goodbye, Sis 27
Enter Jane #2 31
Life Got in the Way… Temporarily 35
Life Must Go On 37
My Next Adventure 47
Just When I Thought Skydiving Couldn't Get Any Better… 53
The Pre-Jump Expedition 59
The Jump 67
Miscellaneous Observations About My North Pole Trip 75
Good Friday Was Especially Good to Me 79
In Between the Good Fridays 83
Good Friday Episode #3 89
Interesting (Curious?) Stuff About Bob 91
Optimistic Bob 99

Acknowledgements

I thank, especially, God, for making my life what it is!

I thank my wife, Jane, without whose encouragement this book would never have been written. Thanks, Jane, for putting up with my stuttering, my hardness of hearing, and my forgetfulness. I love you.

To my son and daughter, Rob and Dawn. I am so proud of your accomplishments. I love you.

To my brother, John, thank you for being a positive influence in my life.

I want to thank Brian Worrell, who taught me the art of selling insurance and how to invest wisely in the product for my family.

To my lifelong friend, Tim Connor, for giving me the phone number for skydiving. Thank you.

Thank you, Gerald "Butch" Myers, for all those crazy jumps we did in our early years of skydiving.

Randy Schroeder, thanks for putting me in touch with Handsome Dave, who had my rig apart and shipped for repair and then reassembled in time for the North Pole jump. And an even bigger thank you to Bill Booth and the North Pole trip organizer's company, for making the repair in such a timely manner. With much gratitude, Bill. Your guidance made the North Pole trip safe and brought me back alive.

To Ken Plankenhorn, my parachute rigger, you saved my life eight times by packing my reserve correctly. It opened every time!

Hats off to all the countless people I have jumped with throughout my twenty-five years of skydiving. You are my friends for life. Thanks for all the good times, and "Blue skies!"

Thank you to my friend, Earl "Rocky" Radabaugh, from whom I learned to be forever young. I loved you, man. You are missed!

To Stephanie Beavers, who took all our notes and conversations, and put them into a readable format for this book. You are excellent. Thanks a million!

Introduction

My name is Bob Atkins. I am seventy-three years old and have been wanting to tell my story for a number of years. Some people would say my story is one of hard luck. I envision them shaking their heads, amazed at the blows I've been dealt and wondering how I've had the strength to get up every morning. To them I say, "It's fine. I'm doing well, thanks." The sun still rises and sets daily. And I have been blessed to have two amazing children—something I consider to be my most important achievement ever.

We all look at life through a different lens. Have difficult events occurred in my life? Yes. Are they any more, or less, worse than events that befall others? Maybe. But, I tell my story here not to seek sorrow or sympathy. I want, instead, to open people's eyes to what is possible when you live life and face each day with positivity—regardless of what appear to be obstacles popping up at every bend in the road. I say "what *appear* to be obstacles" because whether they truly are obstacles is debatable. The Merriam-Webster dictionary defines the word *obstacle* as something that impedes progress or achievement. Being a glass-half-full kind of guy, I prefer to look at obstacles as opportunities, as challenges that present themselves and possibly force a change in the way things are done. I might even argue that an obstacle can be a good thing in that it requires me to go a different way to achieve progress or reach a goal. As a result, I have never looked back and asked why certain events occurred. Nor have I spent time crying over things that cause others to wither and shrivel away. Instead, I put on a different set of glasses and continue to look straight ahead, only now the view in front of me is a changed perspective.

I honestly don't know how unique my situation is. I do know that it's interesting and may even help a few people change their point of view about their own lives. Maybe after reading my story you'll want a new set of glasses too.

PART 1

The Jobs I Loved

This part of my story begins in 1963. I'd just turned seventeen and knew college wasn't in the cards for me. But, boy, was I ready to work. After graduating from high school, I went straight to work at the shoe factory in Myerstown, Pennsylvania, the same place where a lot of people I knew were also employed. I worked in the basement of the building doing piecework on a vulcanizing machine that produced rubber soles for shoes. My pay was $1.15 an hour plus a small amount for each piece I produced—not much for a young man eager to get his feet wet and make a living for himself. The work was pretty easy, and soon I was running four machines at a time. Even so, I was only able to produce a set number of pieces in an eight-hour workday, which kept my earnings in check. If I wanted to make more money, I had to exceed the daily production requirements, which was hard to do. In time, I learned how to run ten machines at once, and doing that proved more fruitful. My pay was bumped up to $1.65 an hour and my production increased considerably just by handling all those machines.

I lasted at the shoe factory for one year—until I got word from my father that the Bethlehem Steel plant in nearby Lebanon was hiring. That was *the* place to work. Bethlehem Steel Corporation paid well—more than most other large employers in the area, so, when openings occurred, they filled up quickly. I guess I got lucky, though. My father was a general foreman for the company, and when I applied and the hiring folks realized I was Johnny Atkins's son, they signed me on right away. That's the way things worked. But I wasn't about to disappoint. As eager as I was to get my first job out of high school, I was just as eager—maybe even more—to work at Bethlehem Steel. One other factor motivated my ambition. My daughter Dawn had just been born. She was beautiful and meant the world to me. (I still have the commemorative El Producto "It's A Girl!" cigar cannister, including cigars, from when she was born.) Having this job gave me the security I needed to be able to properly take care of my family.

I worked hard. I worked steadily. And I worked to learn as much as I could and be recognized for the good work I did. You see, I hated being the new kid on the block. I wanted to learn the job and be known early on for my work ethic and for doing what was required of me and, naturally, for doing it well.

After fifteen years, my perseverance paid off. I finally achieved the status and recognition I craved and knew I deserved. Without getting technical, I had worked my way up to the top position among the company's rank and file and was promoted to the position of bar roller in the steel mill. The Lebanon plant was the only Bethlehem Steel location in which a roller was not part of management. Regardless, what mattered to me was that I had been selected for a position that required the most skill and highest qualifications of all—and I was, at 33, the youngest person ever to be promoted to that position. With daughter Dawn now a teenager and my second child, son Rob, already 8 years old, making top wages as a roller certainly helped pay the bills.

I loved my job as a roller. I was just one of two in the mill in the position, each of us working a different eight-hour shift. I had what I liked to call *supreme authority*, since no one else besides me knew the work my job entailed. I may not have had the authority to hire and fire employees, but that didn't matter. I loved my job and, for a while, it loved me back.

By the 1970s and 1980s, foreign competition in the steel industry was on the rise and some of Bethlehem Steel's work went to Japan. In addition, technology had changed and the industry in general was evolving in how and where steel was used. The heavy industry products the company made were no longer in demand and competitors stepped in and took their own share of the market. I saw the writing on the wall and had done some advance job searching. When the company closed the Lebanon mill in 1984, I was neither surprised nor unprepared. The entire Bethlehem Steel operation in Lebanon closed permanently in 1985.

Here I was, a 38-year-old blue collar worker with no college degree and a 20-year career in an industry that showed no sign of revival.

I had kids to feed and clothe, a mortgage to pay, and an assortment of other bills and expenses the average married couple racks up. What did I do? I got a job in sales. Insurance sales, no less! I told a friend my plan, and he questioned the logic behind trying to sell insurance to people when the unemployment rate was at 20%. My immediate response to him was, "Well, that leaves another 80% I *can* sell to!" If I didn't go into this with a positive mind, how would I ever expect to succeed? Prudential must have liked what they saw. They took me on in February 1985. I was grateful to have a job and looked forward to this new opportunity. There was, however, one problem. I once again found myself as the new kid on the block. Because I was eager to learn the job and do well, my competitive side kicked in again. I attended Prudential's classes to obtain a license to sell insurance and become fully credentialed. In addition, I took in all the on-the-job training I could get.

As things turned out, I enjoyed selling insurance and I was a natural-born salesman, doing most of my selling by meeting with mom and pops across the kitchen table. I figured I had to sell each customer on three things: first, they had to like me; second, they had to like Prudential; and third, they had to like the product I was selling. My thinking was that, if customers believed in me and the company I represented, why wouldn't they buy insurance? And the fact that I, too, had purchased Prudential insurance for myself and my family made selling it to other families even easier.

By the end of 1985, I doubled what had been, to date, the office record in sales production at $2.2 million. In the eleven months I had been selling insurance, I made $4.4 million in sales. People found me instantly likeable and listened to what I had to say. I may not have had a formal education beyond high school, but I was a natural-born communicator who enjoyed communicating with others. The following year, I was promoted to the position of Sales Manager. Though I preferred face-to-face selling, I accepted the job, knowing it would be a necessary step to the even higher-level positions I aspired to in the company. I worked hard, as usual, and kept my nose to the grindstone.

Life Was Good

By 1988, I was into my second year as sales manager with Prudential. In early August of that year, several people from my office, my boss included, were away at a company-wide conference to celebrate and recognize the top sales people. Had I still been in sales, my wife Janice and I would have also attended the conference, but because I was now the sales manager and not in direct sales, I did not qualify to attend.

Since the boss was away, I took advantage one morning—August 4, to be specific—and lingered over another cup of tea to sit and chat with Janice. I called Janice by her nickname, *Sis*. Everyone did. Janice's younger brother had been unable to pronounce her full name as a child, so he simply called her Sis. The name stuck and remained the nickname she went by the for rest of her life.

Sis and I talked for an hour and a half about stuff, about life, about how everything we'd worked so hard for had finally come together. I had a good job with Prudential. She was working at Hess's department store in Lebanon selling cosmetics. We'd invested in several rental properties, all of which were in good shape. Our daughter Dawn had graduated from college two years earlier and was out on her own, and our son Rob was about to start his senior year in high school. Things were humming along the way they were supposed to.

We checked the kitchen clock and realized it was time to get to work. Sis started at ten and I had to drive to my office in Palmyra. I kissed Sis goodbye and headed out. On the way out the door, I nodded and thought to myself just how good life was.

The Accident

I arrived at my office a little before ten. I poured myself a cup of coffee and got to work on the pile of paperwork on my desk. A half hour into the workday my phone rang. The voice on the other end told me that my wife had been involved in a traffic accident and taken to Hershey Medical Center. At that moment, I didn't think to ask why she hadn't been taken to a closer hospital in Lebanon nor was I given any further detail on the extent of her injury.

The route Sis took to get to her job at the mall had been under construction for some time. One stretch of the route had been inactive for weeks. So long, in fact, that drivers had become accustomed to driving through the area without slowing down or focusing on the construction signs. That early August morning, however, things had changed. Construction had finally started and crews were working and directing traffic, which was crawling in some areas, stopped in others. A tractor trailer driver making his routine run through the area was one of those drivers who had stopped paying attention to the construction zone signs. He didn't notice the workers who were directing traffic. Nor did he see Sis's Mazda RX-7 that was stopped just ahead. Her small car didn't stand a chance.

The fact Sis survived the crash was a miracle. In her case, I use the term *survived* loosely. You see, the impact of the truck into the back end of the Mazda forced it into the car in front of her, which was pushed into the car in front of it, and so on—two more times with the fifth car in the chain reaction being that of a state trooper. The truck bumper was so big, and Sis's car so small, the bumper went through the back glass window and rear-ended the front seat, immediately severing Sis's spinal cord.

At the hospital, I learned more details about the accident and about Sis's condition. I learned that Sis was the only one who had been injured in the crash—another miracle—and that, given the extent of her injuries, she had been taken to the medical center in an air ambulance. She was in critical condition and not expected to live. But she did. In an instant, that August 4, 1988, her life and ours together changed forever. She was now a quadriplegic.

Within a month, the doctors at Hershey arranged to have Sis moved, via air ambulance, to the Shepherd Center in Atlanta, Georgia, where she remained from early September to about mid-January 1989. I flew on board along with Sis and the medical team. Shepherd Center provides rehabilitation services to people who have suffered a spinal cord injury. From my experience, I feel Shepherd is the greatest spinal center in the world. The care and treatment Sis received for the time she was there was amazing, something for which I will be forever grateful.

I was also grateful to my employer, who let me work flexible hours during the week so that I could drive down to visit Sis on the weekends. I drove down to Georgia on a Friday, stayed the weekend in an apartment across the street from the hospital, and returned home to Pennsylvania the following Monday. The trip was 750 miles each way, but I thought nothing of it. I had to see Sis. I had to be there with her. And, if she was ever to return home again, I had to learn how to care for her.

Caring for a quadriplegic is tricky business—not like caring for someone who is bedbound with a broken leg. A quadriplegic must rely on other human beings to care for every single aspect of their life: hygiene, food and meal preparation, transportation, home exercises and therapy, medical appointments—everything a fully functioning human being takes for granted. A caregiver must learn to perform catheterization and understand the patient's bowel process—two functions that are vital to a quadriplegic's everyday life. Improper management could lead to a spike in blood pressure and cause the patient to have headaches, nausea, sweating, clammy skin, and worse. Because quadriplegics are incapable of controlling their blood pressure, this is what scared me the most. Regular monitoring was critical. The bottom line for me was that I could never take a day, or even a minute, off from caring for Sis.

And so, on my weekend visits to Atlanta, I learned to do it all. Sis was initially on a ventilator because she was paralyzed from the shoulders down. From there up, she was completely normal. She could think straight and talk just as she always had. In fact, her mental state was fabulous, considering her circumstances (if you can believe that). On one visit, I told Sis about the trials and tribulations Rob and I were having back at home. Sis had always done all the cooking. I didn't know the first thing about putting a meal together. Rob must've been hungry, because he went into the kitchen one night, determined to cook macaroni and cheese for dinner. I decided to help and boiled the water to cook the noodles. I still recall our conversation. "Rob, how much macaroni should I put in the pot?" He responded, "Just dump the whole box in." As you can imagine, we had enough cooked macaroni to feed an army!

My own mental state, on the other hand, was not as good as my wife's. I was angry. Everything had been so good. Our home life and family had been going so well and then the accident happened through no fault of our own. But I was determined to take the best care of Sis that I could. Once she was weaned off the ventilator and able to breathe on her own, and once I proved to her medical team that I could properly take care of her, she was allowed to spend a weekend with me in my Atlanta apartment. That was January 1989. We got through that weekend just fine, so the next big step was to get Sis back to Pennsylvania.

We flew, once again, via air ambulance. In preparation for Sis's return home, I had purchased a van, sight unseen, from a place in

New Mexico, where they did the specialized work of converting the van to accommodate a handicapped person like Sis. The van was ready and waiting for us at the airport when we arrived.

Back home, I took a month off from work to get Sis and myself acclimated to what had become our new way of life—Sis relying on me literally minute by minute for her every need, and me knowing nothing more than the fact I had to take care of my wife, and to try to keep her comfortable and ease her physical burden as much as humanly possible. My boss realized I would not be able to focus on selling insurance with my constant preoccupation about my situation with Sis, so he did not penalize me for the time I took off.

To return to my job selling insurance, I had to have nursing care for Sis the hours I was away at my appointments, which were often evening hours. That had become our new normal. I was either working or I was with Sis, constantly monitoring her condition, her blood pressure, her catheter. I took her to all her regular doctor appointments and also to the hospital on an emergency basis more than once. Sis was highly susceptible to illness, in spite of the precautions I took to keep her well. For any issue that arose that could worsen and negatively affect her health, I put Sis in the van and drove her to Hershey Medical Center, nearly twenty miles away, to have her checked out. (The hospital in Lebanon was not capable of caring for a quadriplegic.) That happened about once a month. The people at the hospital thought I was an attorney because I didn't take no for an answer. I knew what I wanted and what Sis needed, and I made sure they knew.

That spring, Sis and I attended Rob's high school graduation. Sis and Rob had a close relationship, and she was so proud to see her son graduate and move on to the next phase of his life, college. Rob went to Penn State, about a two-hour drive from our home. As a freshman, Rob did not have a car on campus, so I went and picked him up every Friday and brought him home for his weekend visits with Sis. (By the time Rob was a senior, he had his own car to travel back and forth.) Sis's face lit up every time Rob walked into the room. Another special event for Sis was our daughter's wedding, set for December of that same year. Sis was a beautiful mother of the bride, dressed in a Christmas outfit, her hair and nails done to perfection. And so our life continued. We led as normal a family life as we could.

The Stroke

I remember the day well: June 18, 1991. I had wrapped up an appointment to sell car insurance and was driving back home. Along the way, I had trouble seeing. I pulled to the side of the road and thought, "Now what?" I looked in the mirror and noticed my right eyeball had flipped up. (There's no other way to describe what had happened.) So, I covered my eye with one hand and drove the rest of the way home using just the other hand. I thought I probably needed to eat, that maybe my blood sugar was low. Back home, I made myself some food, but was feeling strange. I looked in the mirror and saw that I looked okay. Sis was out with her nurse for a doctor's appointment in Hershey, but after a while, my son came home. I tried to talk to him, but was unable to utter a word. I then realized I'd suffered a stroke. I was unable to speak or read. I couldn't even write the three letters of my own name! When Sis returned from her appointment, Rob told her I was acting strange and that I couldn't talk. I looked at Sis and just shrugged my shoulders as if to say something strange was going on. Sis knew immediately, and she and her nurse took me to the emergency room. They admitted me to the hospital right away.

In the month leading up to the stroke, I'd had physical trouble—pain—on three separate occasions. Each time, the pain was different. The first incident was pain in my stomach, though I had no idea why. I had always been unusually healthy and never sick. I didn't even have a regular doctor. But the stomach pain was enough to cause me to go to an urgent care facility. There, they performed an overall physical examination and I was deemed to be in excellent health. The stomach pain had abated and the doctors attributed it to cramps. The second incident was pain in my leg. Since the urgent care doctor had told me I was in perfect health, I decided to go to a different doctor about the leg pain. By the time I arrived, however, the pain had stopped. A week later, which was the week before the stroke, I had pain in my wrist. Understand, for me to go to the doctor at all, the pain had to have been severe, which it was—in all three cases. The doctor who saw me about the wrist pain told me I had carpal tunnel syndrome. I was wary of the diagnosis and reiterated to the doctor that I had never been sick a day in my life, and here I was, sick three times in three weeks. The doctor said the incidents were unrelated. He prescribed a wrist brace and sent me on my way. I wore the brace for just a day or two.

The fourth health scare was the stroke. That one the doctors took seriously. After all the poking, prodding, and testing, they determined I had acute endocarditis. Simply put, in endocarditis, clumps of bacteria travel to a person's heart and attach to heart chambers or heart valves. These clumps, called vegetations, can break loose and travel to other parts of the body. The three instances of acute pain I had suffered were caused by vegetations that had moved through my body. The fourth instance of traveling vegetation led to a major complication in that it traveled to my brain and caused a blockage which caused the stroke.

I remained in the hospital for ten days. After that, I was back home, receiving intravenous antibiotics for six weeks. I lost all ability to taste, thanks to the antibiotics. All food tasted the same—like nothing! I lost weight and downed nutrition drinks in an effort to keep my weight up. My speech and my ability to read, write, and process simple instructions were still affected. I attended speech therapy and recall one of my early visits. The therapist placed a cigar box on the table in front of me. The box contained a variety of items—a pen, pencil, key, comb, etc.—which she dumped onto the table. She said, "Put the pencil in the box." I thought, no problem, and did as instructed. She next instructed me, "Put the pen and the pencil in the cigar box." I looked at the therapist and then at the pen and the pencil on the table. I knew what she was saying, but I could not complete the task. I was physically incapable of executing these two simple steps. That day, I went home exhausted. Therapy lasted about six weeks, until I decided I no longer wanted to go. My reasoning for suspending the sessions was that I could just as easily work on similar tasks at home. In fact, better therapy for me was going for coffee with a friend and shooting the breeze.

As a result of the stroke, I lost my job selling insurance. I had gone from being a top-producing salesman who loved talking with clients and calculating insurance figures and logically presenting all the benefits of buying insurance to someone who had lost the capacity to process information, read, write, or speak. The last day I sold insurance was June 18, 1991—the day of my stroke. The good thing for me is that I believed in the products I sold. I always thought that, to be successful in sales, you had better use or own the product you're selling, which I did. My company's disability benefits kicked in, and then other insurance policies I had purchased supplemented my income. That allowed me to continue to provide Sis the full level of care she needed by bringing in round-the-clock nursing care until I recovered enough from my stroke to take care of her again.

Recovery was slower and longer than I wanted or expected. Over time, I regained my ability to function, to dress, to eat and speak—to communicate in general. At first, I was unable to drive. I hired a driver to help me run routine errands such as grocery shopping and going to the bank and post office. After about one month, I figured I was well enough to drive. I decided to venture out to the grocery store, but brought my son, Rob, along with me in case I needed help with something. We made it there just fine. I thought, "Piece of cake." I should have held that thought, because trouble came after we were done shopping and ready to leave the parking lot. Apparently, my brain did not yet have the capacity to recall every step I needed to complete when backing a vehicle out of a parking space. Driving forward was not a problem, but driving backwards was a different matter. I did not remember I was supposed to turn around and look in both directions before backing the car up. As a result, I almost backed into someone who was behind my car. Such a simple step, yet my brain did not recall that I needed to do it. I admitted that I probably should not have been driving and handed the keys over to Rob to drive us back home. Thankfully, as my health improved, so did my driving.

Some people who suffer a stroke are so devastated by their condition that they stop doing what they should to really take care of themselves. A defeatist attitude leaves them feeling they just won't be able to better themselves or improve their circumstances, and so they give up. I viewed my stroke differently, just as I did Sis's accident and condition—as blips along our life paths. Not that I'm minimizing quadriplegics and stroke victims, not by a long shot. Sis and I both suffered life-altering, life-threatening events. But we each had to decide how we were going to live going forward—the figurative stance we would take on our respective state of affairs. Were we going to whine and cry and moan day in and day out, feeling sorry for ourselves about our pathetic situations? I already mentioned that Sis's state of mind was amazing, given the fact she had to rely, every second of every day, on another human being to care for her every need and to keep her alive. She had already "been there, done that," as they say, and made the conscious choice to remain positive in the face of her dire circumstances. In my case, and as much as I admired Sis and her upbeat attitude, I did not feel an ounce of self-pity as a result of my stroke. Self-pity is not in my nature; it's not in my genes. You get up every morning and you keep going. In our own way, Sis and I each recognized our health and physical issues for what they were. But we were also ready to deal with them and whatever fallout accompanied them.

Before you go thinking I'm nothing but a foolish optimist, let me tell you about the anger I felt at my situation. Till the day of my stroke, I believed I'd been handling Sis's situation about as well as could be expected. Everything seemed under control. After the stroke, I was no longer able to help my wife as much or as well as I had been doing to that point. Suddenly, I felt overwhelmed. I met with a therapist about eight times, and the therapist put me on an antidepressant. I learned my feelings of anger and helplessness were a form of depression, and that most stroke victims feel depressed following a stroke. In time and with God's grace, I got through and survived my depression.

My recovery has been long and slow. I say *has been* because I'm still recovering, even though nearly thirty years have passed since my stroke. Where I once completed forms and handled piles of paperwork as a successful insurance salesman, today I avoid anything that involves filling out a form. The information is just too much for my brain to process. And, for a long time, the immediate aftereffects of the stroke had me thinking hard about every word that came out of my mouth. That was exhausting work. To this day, words still escape me and speaking is, at times, difficult. Where I always enjoyed talking in front of people and presenting to a group, I no longer do. I shy away from group conversations and rarely talk on the phone. I much prefer speaking one on one. On the bright side, I feel I'm better off listening than talking because, when you listen, you learn.

The Seizure

I ended Sis's round-the-clock nursing care about two months after my stroke. By then I was well enough to handle her care at night, even though I still relied on nursing help during the day. One night, in January 1992, Sis and I were home alone. My memory remains fuzzy, but it was either late night or very early morning, and we were asleep in bed. Then it happened. I had a grand mal seizure. The violent muscle contractions I was experiencing were enough to wake Sis up. She knew right away what was happening and used the only tool available to her—her voice. Over and over, Sis said, "Bob, you're having a seizure. Call Betty Lou." Betty Lou was a neighbor, who also happened to be a nurse.

"Bob, you're having a seizure. Call Betty Lou."

"Bob, you're having a seizure. Call Betty Lou."

"Bob, you're having a seizure. Call Betty Lou."

Finally, I woke up enough to hear my wife's words, and made the call to Betty Lou. I don't know how long my seizure lasted, and I could have lost consciousness. Miraculously, I emerged from the seizure, though I was confused and disoriented. I now heard clearly, "Bob, you're having a seizure. Call Betty Lou. Bob, you're having a seizure. Call Betty Lou." In my dream-like state, I was conscious enough to hear Sis's words and do what she instructed. I called Betty Lou, who immediately called an ambulance for me.

The ambulance crew arrived and took care of me. At one point, they said I had suffered the worst seizure they had ever seen. Imagine the terror Sis must have felt knowing I was having a seizure and she was completely powerless to do anything about it. I have never had another seizure since, and this one appears to have been triggered by my stroke. Had I lost consciousness or not come out of the seizure, Sis and I surely would have died right there in our bed.

Sis's Dream Trip

The incident with my seizure came and went. I had few aftereffects and was able to return to our "normal" life. My next plan was to take Sis to Hawaii. She had always wanted to travel there, and I wanted to make her dream trip a reality. I knew, however, that I could not take Sis on such a long trip on my own. I would need help. I had recently hired a nurse, Jane, full-time. Jane had originally come to us from an agency, and, from the moment she first came into our home, she and Sis really got along. I liked Jane too, and thought, "Why not just bring her on full-time?" Jane agreed. She left the agency and came to work for us directly.

And so we traveled to Hawaii in April 1992—me, Sis, and Jane. The plan was to stay in Maui for thirty days. I rented an apartment that accommodated a handicapped person and a handicapped van to drive us around. I took Sis out to dinner and fed her myself. People were curious and they looked at Sis and me doing our thing. I can't tell you if they approved or disapproved of a handicapped woman at a restaurant being spoon-fed by her husband, but I didn't care. Sis didn't care either. She was beyond thrilled with the whole experience. I even flew our son Rob out for a week. He was on spring break from college and happy to join us. Sis and I traveled first-class all the way. I wanted to make sure she had the best time she could. She did, in spite of her paralysis and all the limitations that went with it. I was happy with the whole trip just knowing how much Sis enjoyed it. (In case you're wondering, nurse Jane flew in coach class!)

Goodbye, Sis

On my weekend drives back and forth to the Shepherd Center in Georgia when Sis was first injured, I used the hours spent on the long, lonely stretch of highway between Charlotte, North Carolina, and Atlanta to think and pray. On one of those drives, I prayed to God, "When will it be over? When will Sis show signs of recovery? When will she improve?" Whether you doubt me or believe me, I heard a response to those pleadings, and the response I heard was "June 26." That conversation with God took place in 1988.

When I reached the hospital, I told Sis about my conversation with God and about the response He gave me of "June 26." I looked for improvement on June 26, 1989; again on June 26, 1990; and so on. Every June 26, I looked for Sis to show a sign of improvement. No improvement ever came.

Sis was in and out of the hospital numerous times with blood pressure spikes or some other concern. In April 1993, Sis contracted bronchitis and was admitted to the hospital on April 15. The bronchitis turned into pneumonia, which stuck with her for weeks. Sis's condition continued to deteriorate and she soon had to be back on a ventilator. She never regained enough health to return home, and passed away peacefully on Thursday, June 24, 1993.

I was prepared for Sis's passing, but, at the same time, unprepared. I had watched as Sis's condition worsened and in my heart knew she was leaving us. Lord knows I wanted her to be out of her pain and discomfort; nonetheless, when she passed she took a piece of my heart with her.

Rob was away at school and due home the following day. I decided to wait until he returned home on Friday night to tell him that his mother had passed away. I knew he would be devastated. In the end, I did not have to have that conversation with him. Rob knew what had happened the minute he walked in the door. You see, he normally arrived home each weekend to an empty house, as I was always at the hospital with Sis. That night, however, he saw my car in the driveway and knew I was home. The look on my face told Rob all he needed to know.

The next day, Rob and I went to a funeral home to pick out a casket. Nurse Jane, who had been taking care of Sis at home and spending time with her in the hospital, including the night Sis died, happened to be in the area and saw us in the funeral home parking lot. She pulled into the lot and we chatted for a few minutes. Jane and Sis had been close—friends, actually—and Jane knew all about Sis's family. She asked, "Does Sis's mother know?" Sis's mother, Eleanor, was in a nursing home after having suffered a stroke and being paralyzed on one side. In my grief, I had forgotten to tell Eleanor about Sis's passing.

That afternoon, Rob and I went to see Eleanor. Amazingly, she knew Sis had died before I had a chance to tell her, just as had occurred with Rob. Upon seeing me, Eleanor said, "I had a dream about Sissy. She was running and playing. She was whole again."

I was struck by Eleanor's words and knew in my heart and soul that what, to her, was a dream, was actually a vision. The date of that conversation was Saturday, June 26, the date God had given me five years earlier on my drive to see Sis in the hospital in Atlanta. God had given me the date Sis was made whole again—in Heaven. With the realization that Sis was in Heaven, I had finally found some peace for myself.

Enter Jane #2

About two months after Sis's passing, in August 1993, I was at home, seated at my desk and feeling sorry for myself. I struggled with the loss of Sis and having to live on my own. Without Sis, I had no reason to be happy. I had never lived alone and did not like waking up every morning with only the dog to talk to. Sis and I had had frank and open conversations about how I would live the rest of my life if she died before me. Sis knew me well. She knew I would not last long alone and gave me her full blessing to remarry, if that is what made me happy. I later researched the topic of a surviving spouse who remarries instead of staying single. I learned something interesting. Experts on the topic say that a man who gets married again after his wife dies, in effect, honors her, and the new union is a symbol of the man's enjoyment of his married life with the deceased spouse. The message for those who remain behind was clear: life must go on.

That particular August day, I recalled one of Sis's other caregivers, also named Jane, just like the nurse I formerly employed. This Jane worked multiple jobs, and had come in only sporadically to care for Sis. In addition to working as a nurse, Jane also worked as a massage therapist and a realtor. She usually came to care for Sis from six to nine o'clock when I had to go to evening sales appointments. Jane and I had what we later called a "Hi"-"Bye" relationship, since we saw each other only in passing when she was coming and I was going. I remembered Jane specifically, because she worked closely with Sis, giving her neck and shoulder massages to ease her pain. You might wonder how it is possible for a person with a severed spinal cord to feel pain. Pain of this type is called phantom pain. Phantom pain most likely occurs as a result of tangled sensory wires causing mixed messages to be sent to the brain. Sis once told me, "I can deal with the paralysis. But then along came this phantom pain." When the pain is musculoskeletal, therapeutic massage is usually a recommended treatment. Sis looked forward to the temporary relief the massages gave her. And she became friendly with Jane, too, often discussing home and family events.

After thinking about Sis, her pain, and the massages that eased the pain, I thought about Jane. Even though Jane and I had hardly spoken more than two words to each other in the weeks and months she came to give Sis her massages, I wondered if she would be interested in going on a date with me. I came up with what I thought was a good plan for calling Jane. I didn't know if she knew that Sis had died, so I told her I wanted to tell her something important about the date of June 26. To get my foot in the door, literally, I also made an appointment for a massage. When I went to Jane's in-home office, I learned that Jane had already heard about Sis's passing, so she was not surprised at the news. She was sad, though, and listened quietly as I recounted the story of the significance of June 26, clearly a spiritual sign for me.

At the end of my appointment, I asked Jane for a date. She said no. I asked her a second time, and again she said no. "Why?" I asked. She explained that she did not date her clients. Well, a person who had been a successful insurance salesman does not take no for an answer. Without being overly pushy to the point of obnoxious, I told her I did not want any more massages, which meant I was no longer her client. I asked her out a third time, which was the charm. Jane relented and we soon went on our first date.

I wanted to make a good impression. Dinner at an expensive restaurant was my plan. And, I wanted to look good for my date. I bought a new sports coat for the occasion and thought I would further impress Jane if I picked her up in my '92 Corvette ZR-1. On the drive over, I noticed I had not removed the tag that was sewn onto the jacket sleeve. "Oh, great," I thought. Picking up a woman for a first date while wearing a jacket with the manufacturer's tag still on the sleeve would not make the best first impression. So, I pulled the car over and sat there until I pulled out every last thread that had been keeping the tag in place. Problem solved.

Over dinner, Jane and I made the usual first-date chit chat. One thing I needed to know was how she leaned politically, because I probably would not have been able to date a woman whose political views were opposite my own. Once we got that conversation out of the way, we enjoyed our drinks and our dinner and both agreed our first date went "pretty good." Jane confided later that she did not know what to think when she saw me pull up in a bright aqua Corvette, though she was impressed and thought I looked handsome.

Life Got in the Way… Temporarily

My son, Rob, was spending a semester abroad as a requirement of his college studies in international trade. I decided to take advantage while Rob was in Europe to visit him and see a bit of Europe on the side. I had made these travel plans before my first date with Jane, and the trip ended up being a two-week whirlwind tour. At the same time, Jane had travel plans of her own. She and a cousin were traveling to Scotland, England, and Wales for ten days, and leaving before I was scheduled to return home. In my ongoing quest to impress Jane, I decided to call her from London to wish her well on her trip. "And be careful crossing the streets," I told her. "They drive on the wrong side of the road here!" Jane laughed at the comment and admitted to me later that she had decided then and there that dating me would be just fine.

For my return flight from Europe—London to New York—I decided to fly on a Concorde jet. I thought it would be fun to fly the supersonic airliner so that, time-wise, I would land back home before I left! The aircraft was incredible. There was no first class or coach class—all the seats were the same. I was one of the fortunate few on the plane who got to just sit back and enjoy the flight. Everyone else around me seemed to be working or conducting some sort of business! They didn't know what they were missing. At mealtime, passengers were served on china and given real silverware to use. Fine dining in the air! The lunch-dinner menu was equally impressive, and I recall eating fresh papaya and roast lamb with mushrooms and potatoes. I may have had a glass of wine to accompany the entrée, but I don't remember. Dessert was a lemon mousse and then they served cheese and *crudité* before ending the meal with coffee and chocolates. I had to laugh because they also offered sandwiches for folks who wanted them instead of the full meal. Sandwiches! I don't think so. When flying on a Concorde, you need to get the whole experience, and eating from a menu that matches the menu of any four-fork restaurant in Manhattan is definitely part of that experience.

The plane flew at an altitude of 60,000 feet (about 11.3 miles) and a speed of Mach 2, which is twice the speed of sound—over 1,300 miles per hour. At that speed, the flight home was half the time of a normal flight. The aircraft was so high up, the sky was black and we could see the curvature of the earth. A screen on the bulkhead showed relevant flight data. I was especially surprised to see that the outside temperature was around -70°F. For a number of reasons, the Concorde is no longer in use, so I'm glad I had the opportunity to fly on one when I did.

Life Must Go On

Jane and I dated for about four months when I decided it was time to see how compatible we would be as travel companions. Jane was up for a trip, and we decided on Rio de Janeiro, Brazil. In early December 1993, we went to the local AAA office to get help organizing our travel plans. The employee at AAA asked, "Why Rio?" Jane and I explained simply that Rio was a place we'd both always wanted to visit. The woman suggested we take our trip to Ixtapa, on the west coast of Mexico. We hadn't given any prior thought to traveling to Mexico, but Jane and I discussed her recommendation briefly and trusted her judgement enough to take her up on it. The woman looked back and forth at us and, with a knowing look, said, "Ixtapa will be where you spend your honeymoon." At those words, Jane and I looked at each other, shrugged, and said in unison, "Yeah, right." Jane and I agreed and booked our trip for February.

Almost as if on cue, just three weeks after our visit to AAA—on Christmas Eve—I proposed to Jane. I rounded out my proposal by giving her a rock—a two-carat diamond ring. Jane, of course, thought the ring was too big and was embarrassed by the size of it. She accepted my proposal and later told me that, when at work at her job in the real estate office, she turned the ring around on her finger to hide the diamond.

At this point, I want to reiterate just how deeply I loved Sis. I put my entire life on hold to take care of her. In fact, if I had to do it all over again, I would. In the end, though, Sis understood me and wanted me to resume what she knew would be a normal, full life for myself. She would not have been happy any other way. I feel it was with Sis's blessing that Jane and I got married in February 1994, not quite two months after I proposed, and barely six months after our first date. Our wedding took place at the Hotel Hershey. The ceremony was perfect—small and simple. And, sure enough, we honeymooned in Ixtapa, just like the AAA woman said!

Jane came into our marriage with three children and I had two. I had always wanted five children and Jane helped my wish come true. When we were first married, Jane moved into the house I had shared with Sis and our children. Over time, I realized Jane was probably not happy living in the home of my first wife. We decided to remain in the same neighborhood, but build a home that represented the start of our new life together. As much as I loved Sis, I also love Jane. Jane accepted me for who I was, as I continued to carry the aftereffects of the stroke I had suffered two years earlier. And she does to this day, some twenty-five years later.

PART 2

PART 2

Bob on the North Pole

Ice airport at the North Pole

Russian roommates in Khatanga (Bob is second from right)

Tailgate of Russian IL-76 jet from which Bob jumped to parachute to the North Pole

Small notebook where Bob noted details of the North Pole expedition (Bob's writing was slow after his stroke; he took 30 minutes to write one small page)

Fellow parachutists at the North Pole

Skydiving in a raft

Bob making a smooth landing

Skydivers in *VT* formation

Bob (in white suit) participating in a four-way jump

Jumpers Over Seventy – JOS

Bob, today, in his home office surrounded by mementos of what matter most to him: family and skydiving

My Next Adventure

By now you have probably gathered that, for me, the glass is always at least half full. Not much holds me back, and I don't listen to naysayers. I love life and every day is a new adventure and a new reason to get out of bed in the morning. Little did I know, in early July 1994, the amazing turn my life would take.

I was having coffee with a friend one morning, and the subject of skydiving came up. I had always been interested in skydiving, but did not know the first thing about it. My friend mentioned that another mutual friend of ours, Tim, did skydiving. That same day I called Tim, who told me he had done a few jumps. I told him I was interested in learning the sport. "How do you go about getting started as a skydiver?" I asked. Tim suggested I call the Chambersburg Municipal Airport (known today as the Franklin County Regional Airport). No sooner did Tim and I hang up from our call than I made a second call—to the airport to sign up to take my first jump course the following Wednesday, July 6.

That same day, Rob called and told me he was coming home for a visit. I was glad to know my son was coming home, and I was also excited to tell him my news. "Wait'll you hear what I just signed up for," I said. Rob asked what. "A skydiving lesson." There was silence on the other end for about ten seconds. Rob wasn't sure how to react to my latest venture, or, should I say, *ad*venture. Here was his old man, still dealing with stuttered speech as a remnant of the stroke, getting ready to go up in a plane and jump out. "Really, Dad? You're serious?" "One hundred percent," I said. Rob knew nothing would stop me. So, in an if-you-can't-beat-'em-join-'em moment, he said, "Sign me up too."

The big day came, and Rob and I headed to Chambersburg Airport for the six-hour ground school class. The best part, however—and what I looked forward to all day—was what I'll call the practicum: an actual jump at the end of the day after the six hours of ground school were completed. During the practicum, three of us went up in the plane. Now, most students, especially those on their very first jump, jump in tandem with another more experienced (certified) skydiver or instructor. In a tandem jump, the student is attached to the instructor by a special harness, and the instructor guides the student through the entire jump. Even though I was nervous at the thought of doing my first jump, I was equally anxious to learn without being encumbered by either a harness or being attached to another jumper. The instructors allowed me to do what is called an accelerated free fall, or AFF. In AFF, two instructors accompany the student on his or her free fall jump, which is made at 10,500 feet. Each instructor holds on to the student's harness. This keeps the student stable, so the student can demonstrate their knowledge of skydiving skills such as free fall body position, landing procedures, and emergency procedures. Today, some twenty-five years after my first jump, AFF has become the most common method used to train people on how to skydive.

I know I was an attentive student during the ground class. I also know we discussed free fall in great detail, but I can honestly say that, until you actually experience free fall for yourself, you really have no idea what it is. Being pulled to earth by the force of gravity while simultaneously experiencing air resistance in opposition to the downward movement is like no other feeling on earth. The sensation was—and continues to be to this day—amazing. I do admit to getting nauseous the first couple of times out. That occurred because of the rocking of the parachute. As I gained experience, nausea soon became a thing of the past.

Believe it or not, my original intent was to go to the Chambersburg Airport and jump once, and only once. (Once was enough for my son!) But I scheduled a second jump, and a third, and I haven't looked back since. Skydiving got into my blood and I completely and absolutely fell in love with the sport. I started out jumping once a week, and decided I wanted to get licensed. The United States Parachute Association (USPA) awards four licenses: A, B, C, D. Each license requires a certain number of jumps be met, currently 25, 50, 200, 500, respectively, in addition to a series of other requirements. In 1994, the A license requirement was 20 jumps, which was my goal. Wasting no time, I earned my A license in just two months.

I've met people who don't find skydiving to be that big of a deal. "It's only a jump," they say. Only a jump? Hardly. When jumping at 12,000–13,000 feet, you start out with less oxygen. The evaporation of the moisture from your skin when you're in free fall dehydrates you and makes you tired. And, afterwards, packing the parachute back into its container can take anywhere from fifteen to thirty minutes. I don't think about the physical aspect of skydiving. I only know that, for the sixty seconds I'm in free fall, nothing else matters. I block out everything and enjoy (yes, *enjoy*) the intensity of the moment. Over the past twenty-five years I've been doing skydiving, I guess you could say I've gotten "pretty good" at the sport.

I was forty-eight years old when I made my first jump—not exactly a kid. As usual, I didn't like being the inexperienced one. I wanted to learn as much as I could, and so I kept at the sport, enjoying it more each time I jumped. On the days I went skydiving at the Chambersburg Airport, some eighty-four miles from home one way, I wanted to make at least six jumps to make the drive worth it—and that's exactly how I planned my days. The added benefit for me has always been the camaraderie among skydivers, which, for me, is what I love most about skydiving. One typical event I always enjoy attending is what is called a boogie. A boogie is, literally, a skydiving party. When a boogie is called, lovers of the sport gather to jump at a designated drop zone, and afterwards have a beer or two (or more) and share stories of skydiving experiences. A boogie is a great way to meet fellow skydivers and both indulge in, and enjoy, the fun of the sport together. Skydiving has allowed me to make hundreds of new friends. Any differences there might be between us are irrelevant. I could be on the same plane load with a surgeon, a trash collector, a mechanic, a vice president of a major corporation. I now have close women friends—something that was unimaginable to me prior to taking up the sport. Nothing matters—not education level, not economic status, not the fact a person stutters because of a stroke. When we skydive, we are all the same.

Just When I Thought Skydiving Couldn't Get Any Better...

As a member of the United States Parachute Association, one of my perks was to receive their official monthly publication called *Parachutist*. I enjoyed reading the magazine from cover to cover, as I was interested in learning as much as I could about my new-found passion for skydiving. In the October 1994 issue, I saw an advertisement for a skydiving expedition from Moscow to the North Pole being organized for the following spring—specifically, the jump would take place on Easter Sunday (April 16, 1995), or as close to that day as possible.

"I have to do this jump," I told Jane. The truth was, nothing was going to stop me. Thank goodness Jane did not object. Her thinking was that anyone, including me with my post-stroke stammering speech, should be able to do whatever we feel we are meant to do in life. Even knowing the risks involved, not only with skydiving, but skydiving on the North Pole after traveling first to Russia and then to Siberia as part of the journey to making the jump, Jane did not give me any grief. In fact, she was wholeheartedly in agreement with my decision to make this trip.

The organizer of the expedition was the legendary Bill Booth of Deland, Florida, engineer and inventor of skydiving equipment that has contributed greatly to improving safety in the sport and earned him awards, recognitions, and accolades from the Parachute Equipment Industry Association and the Fédération Aéronautique Internationale. In other words, if I was going to go skydiving at the North Pole, I was especially happy to know Bill Booth would be running the show.

I answered Bill's magazine ad and received a packet of information a few weeks later. A minimum of 75 jumpers was needed, though Bill was hoping for twice that number. In the end, 126 people went on the expedition, 23 of whom were from the United States. Bill organized the trip such that the Americans were to meet in New York City on April 12, spend one night at a hotel, then all fly to Moscow together the next day out of John F. Kennedy International Airport. The cost for the trip was $4,000 plus the airfare to and from Moscow and cost of special equipment and clothing needed to withstand subzero temperatures. Subzero is an understatement; temperatures on the North Pole could range from –25°C to –40°C, which is –4°F to –40°F. The $4,000 included all food, lodging, and transportation from Moscow to the North Pole and back. Roundtrip airfare to Moscow was about $1,000 and specialty clothing another $1,000. I sent Bill a check for the $500 deposit. The balance due of $3,500 was to be paid in cash—in the form of hundred-dollar bills—which Bill would collect on the

Drawn to the Heavens

Moscow-to-Siberia flight. Imagine 126 people handing all this money over to Bill. That's $441,000 in cash!

Most people might balk or be concerned about having to pay so much in cash and think Bill Booth was going to do something fishy with all that money. But our group of global skydivers was not like most people—we trusted Bill to do the right thing. This was, after all, his fourth trip to the North Pole. Each previous trip required him to rely on the Russians to get his group of skydivers safely there and back, and he had indicated upfront that this was how things needed to be done. He also indicated that we would pay the Russians directly, and that our cash payment covered all food, lodging, and transportation for the Moscow–North Pole–Moscow portion of the trip. He added that a lot of preparation and work by dozens of Russians was necessary to "pave our way."

Side trips could be had for another $50 per person per trip. For example, we might enjoy an excursion that included a day trip flying around Siberia in an Mi-8 transport helicopter, followed by a parachute jump into a Dolgan village. The Dolgan people were, in essence, Eskimos of Mongolian descent who herded reindeer and traded in furs. Another excursion might be to go snowmobiling on one of the rivers and visiting an actual Siberian prison camp. These options might not appeal to most, but I was along for the ride and to get as much out of this once-in-a-lifetime trip that I possibly could.

In case you're wondering, here's how the actual trip to the North Pole was scheduled to occur.

1. The group convenes in Moscow and remains there for two days of sightseeing, including an evening at the Bolshoi Theatre.

2. Fly five hours via a Russian commercial jet from Moscow to the town of Khatanga (pronounced *HOT-en-ga*) on the Taymyr Peninsula in north central Siberia.

3. In Khatanga, wait at the hotel for good enough weather at the North Pole for jumping. April weather is usually good, with surface temperatures at −30°F, light winds, and clear, blue skies, so the wait would not be more than a couple of days at most. While there, take our excursion to the Dolgan village and enjoy a reindeer rib barbecue dinner with the locals.

4. In the meantime, the Russians fly via helicopter to an airbase at the edge of the polar ice cap, where they refuel and then fly as far as possible onto the ice cap. At that location, they set up a manned base and receive the fuel drops that are needed to complete the journey to the pole. Once in the vicinity of the pole, they seek out an area of unbroken ice where they can land, unload a small snow plow, and use the plow to clear a runway one kilometer long. This runway becomes what they refer to as the "ice airport."

5. Next, another ground crew with tents and supplies is transported to the ice airport via a fifty-passenger An-74 jet—an aircraft built to operate in the harshest of weather conditions.

6. At this point, the group is on standby, waiting for word that the weather looks good for jumping. When word comes, everyone boards an IL-76 jet and settles in for the three-hour flight to the pole. While en route to the pole, another Mi-8 helicopter flies from the ice airport to the North Pole, relying on GPS to reach its destination. (One year, the ice airport was 71 kilometers—approximately 44 miles—from the pole.) At the pole, the Russians set up a tent and target area, and await the group's arrival.

7. At the pole, the IL-76 makes four passes: one at 500 feet to calibrate altimeters, one at 1,000 feet to drop cargo, and two at 12,000 feet for the jumpers. Since we were in a transport aircraft, we were to jump from the tailgate, which was wide enough for eight people to jump at one time.

8. Once everyone makes their jump and is accounted for on the pole, the group spends three hours there. At the end of that time, the helicopter makes multiple round trips to and from the pole to the ice airport, to fly groups of twenty-five people at a time back to the ice airport, a trip that could take approximately twenty-five minutes one-way.

9. With everyone back at the ice airport, the group boards the An-74 jet and blasts off from the polar ice cap for the three-hour flight

back to Khatanga (which Bill described as "civilization"), followed by the five-hour trip back to Moscow.

Anything could change those plans at any time. The instability of the Russian economy could make the trip cost more than the $4,000 we were originally charged. The types of any of the aircraft could change, depending on their availability. Bad weather or weather unfavorable to parachuting could cause a delay at every stage. Injury, illness, or some other emergency could preempt an excursion. Etcetera, etcetera, etcetera, up to, and including, a failed jump.

I was raring to go.

The Pre-Jump Expedition

In March 1995, a month before I was scheduled to depart on the North Pole expedition, I was out doing a jump with my friend Butch. That particular day, I forgot to bring my parachute home. (I blame my forgetfulness on memory loss from the stroke!) Butch called me later and told me he had picked up my parachute. "Okay," I said. "I'll get it from you when we jump next week." Butch's dog must have hung around my parachute while Butch had it. I had a dog too, Nikki, and I'm sure Butch's dog sniffed Nikki's scent and left his own scent on the parachute. When I retrieved my parachute, I put it in a closet at home, but Nikki got into the closet where she found—and smelled—my parachute. At that point, she proceeded to chew halfway through the harness. Needless to say, I was furious. I was just three weeks away from departing on the North Pole expedition and my parachute was unusable!

With no time to lose, I called my contact at the Chambersburg Airport, Randy Schroeder, to see what he might suggest. He gave me the name of a rigger in our area, Dave DeWolf. A rigger is someone who is trained to make alterations and repairs to parachutes. This was my first contact with Dave, and we quickly became good friends. Dave is another legendary name in the world of parachuting and rigging. He gained international fame as a parachute rigging instructor and skydiver who accumulated over

13,000 jumps in his lifetime. I called Dave, and he assured me he could help by disassembling the chute and shipping it to Bill Booth's company in Florida, as they had the parts needed for the repair. I was somewhat less optimistic, knowing everything that had to occur in just three weeks' time for me to have an operating parachute. This was unheard of. Normally, repairing a parachute would take three months or longer. In the end, the repair was done in time. Bill facilitated the acceleration of the repair of my parachute, knowing I was going to need it back in time for the North Pole expedition. The repaired parachute was shipped back to Dave DeWolf, who reassembled it and called me in time. I gave both Bill and Dave a big thank you for their help.

Finally, Day 1—the start of my journey on the North Pole skydiving expedition—arrived. At the time, I had accumulated eighty-six jumps and was still in recovery mode from my stroke. Everyone else had made thousands of jumps. By comparison, I was inexperienced, even though I had full confidence in my ability. I arrived in New York City on Wednesday, April 12, and checked in to our designated hotel. Eleven others who were part of the expedition were also at the hotel, as was Bill Booth. (The other Americans on the expedition arrived in New York later that evening.) As much as I knew about Bill and his safety inventions and fame in the world of parachuting, I had never seen a picture of him. I had no idea what the man looked like. Imagine my surprise when he joined the group—he had longish hair and a full beard that was so long it covered his entire chest and then some. I am probably the only one among our group of twelve jumpers and Bill, who, as we had dinner, envisioned images of the Last Supper with Jesus Christ and his twelve disciples seated around the table. Good Friday was just two days away, and that probably helped fuel those thoughts.

The next day, April 13, all twenty-three of us flew together to Moscow, where we connected with the rest of the group. The check-in process at the Hotel Russia took three and a half hours! The hotel was as wide as a city block and six stories high. While waiting to check in, I needed to use the men's room. Imagine my surprise to find the men's room attendant was a woman, and even further surprise to see that the "toilet" was nothing more than a hole in the floor. I did what I needed to do and returned to the lobby as quickly as possible. Thankfully, there was an actual toilet in my room.

Back in the lobby, I changed three hundred American dollars for Russian rubles. At the time, the Russian currency was so devalued, I received a huge stack of bills in exchange. I showed my fellow travelers all the money I'd received, and they immediately told me to put the money away and keep it safely out of sight. The thinking was that Russia in 1995 was like the lawlessness of the American Wild West. I returned home with 78,000 rubles, thinking I might change them back to dollars. I never did, and learned that my 1993 rubles are worthless today.

For breakfast, we all went to the top floor of the hotel where we were served peas and hot dogs (with no buns). As we sat eating breakfast, we watched a lone cat meander among the tables. We thought the meal was strange and their restaurant health code nonexistent, but I did enjoy the tea. In fact, I'd say the Russian tea was great, in spite of the grounds at the bottom of the cup.

I've been asked over the years if I was ever concerned that my speech issues might have negatively affected my experience in terms of being able to full and properly communicate with everyone on the expedition. I was never worried about that. Since most of the other jumpers were from other countries and spoke a different language, I figured we wouldn't have been able to communicate much anyway.

We remained in Moscow until Easter Sunday, April 16, when we departed for Khatanga. If all went as planned, we would be parachuting over the North Pole the following day. On the flight to Khatanga, Bill collected everyone's money and put it in a plain brown paper bag. Each of us had done what Bill instructed: bring $3,500 in hundred-dollar bills ready to be handed over to the Russians. When we landed in Khatanga, we watched as Bill carried the bag of money and gave it to his Russian contact. We took this exchange of cash for services quite seriously, as our lives depended on the help we were to receive from the Russians. Our "hotel" in Khatanga was actually more like a dormitory; it had three floors, with one bathroom per floor. When you do the math, that meant that at least 42 people shared a single bathroom. Not quite the Ritz Carlton! We heard Khatanga had, at one time, been a prison, though not a prison with cells that keep prisoners locked in. There was no need to keep people behind bars in Khatanga, because anyone who attempted to escape would not get very far before freezing to death. It was sure easy to imagine the no-frills dorm we stayed in as once being a prison.

We landed in Khatanga at 11:30 p.m. and went directly to our lodgings. Even though it was late at night, it was not dark. Another jumper, Bill, and I entered our assigned room, only to find three other men already asleep there. Naturally, they heard us enter and woke up. The three men were Russians who were traveling on business; they were not part of our group of jumpers. When they saw Bill and me, they immediately roused from their sleep. One of the men got up and pulled a Bowie knife from his suitcase. Bill and I did not say a word. We then watched another man set out sandwiches, a jar of stewed tomatoes, and a bottle of vodka. The man with the knife stabbed a tomato and held it out in front of me. This Russian was not going to be satisfied until I ate the food he was offering. Stewed tomatoes of all things! And that late at night.

Bill and I did the honorable and polite thing and each ate a sandwich and a tomato and downed a shot of vodka. Well, one shot turned into two, and more. And, the more we drank, the friendlier we all got.

At 2 a.m., I went to the lounge where I ate potatoes and eggs and drank champagne. I was hungry and needed to pass time until 3 a.m., which was the time of a meeting Bill Booth had called. At the meeting, Bill told the group that we would probably be making our North Pole jump within the next 24 hours.

I was fairly wired and excited from all the travel. I didn't really feel like going to bed, but by five o'clock, everything had caught up with me and I lay on my bed and slept for about three hours. By eight, I was ready to get up for good. Back in the lounge, I enjoyed a breakfast of dry bread, Swiss cheese, salami, and more of that fabulous Russian tea.

I was curious to learn as much as I could at every stop on this trip, including about Khatanga. After breakfast, several of us decided to venture out for a walk to see what we might find. There's not much sightseeing to do in a small Siberian village, but we encountered children and others who happily posed for our cameras. Before returning to our dorm for lunch, we met a local man known as Vladimir the Hunter. Vladimir showed up at our dorm later that afternoon, bringing with him some of the results of his hunting adventures. He showed me a gorgeous silver Arctic fox hat. "How much?" I asked, already envisioning Jane wearing the hat. Vladimir indicated an amount equal to $70, which was a bargain. I bought the hat which Jane has stored away to this day.

At a three o'clock briefing, Bill told the group that our jump could take place anywhere between 4:30 p.m. and 8 p.m., and that everyone should get ready to leave. At seven o'clock, word finally came that we would be leaving in one hour. The adrenalin was starting to pump.

The Jump

My mind was working overtime with thoughts of the flight to the pole and of being mentally and emotionally prepped for the jump. Bill reminded us that the North Pole is a mass of constantly shifting ice on top of the Arctic Ocean, and that, with the sun up twenty-four hours a day in early spring, an enormous crack forms that runs through the pole. In my mind, a crack meant water, and the one thing that concerned me most was getting wet. With everything else that could go wrong, I was most afraid of falling through ice and getting wet without anyone nearby to help. In fact, I had serious doubts that I, or any of us, would survive the jump. I suspect others had the same doubts.

The plan was for the jet to make two passes at sufficient elevation for us to jump in two separate groups: half would jump on the first pass, the other half on the second. Each group would be further divided into five groups of ten jumpers. In spite of my nervousness, I wanted to enjoy every single minute—no, every *second*—of this jump, so my roommate Bill and I got in place on the tailgate of the plane to be among the first group to jump. Included in our group would be a Russian, who would jump first, followed by the professional jumpers. In the end, the plan failed, as everything turned to bedlam and it was, literally, every man for himself.

While I stood waiting, a peaceful feeling came over me—a kind of spiritual realization—that indicated I would be just fine and that the jump would go exactly as planned. I said a prayer to thank God for all the love in my live—Jane, Sis, Dawn, and Rob. I also thanked God for his help in making this parachute experience a safe one. Shortly thereafter came an ear-piercing horn blast—our signal that the tailgate was about to open and we were all to jump.

The day was Monday, April 17. The time was near midnight. The jet was flying at 170 to 200 miles per hour. A regular free fall jump occurs at 120 miles per hour—fast enough to fly over one football field per second. When the tailgate opened, I saw the exhaust vapor coming from the four jet engines. Then everyone started jumping. As they exited the plane, their bodies were turning every which way, going end over end. I realized the jet wash was incredibly strong and causing everyone to tumble. I never lost my balance, but the strength of the jet wash threw me almost completely upside down. I straightened out quickly enough, turned just once to look at everyone else, then started to enjoy the freefall.

To this day I am amazed at the pilots' ability to locate the exact jump spot on this enormous piece of floating ice. They can calculate where the pole is, and then five minutes later, it's no longer there. And on the ground, it's easy to get lost. Since the sun rotates around the earth at ten degrees, it is not a reliable guide. At the time we made our jump in 1995, fewer than 2,000 people had ever been to the North Pole.

I was wearing ski goggles, as recommended by Bill, but I also remembered his advice: "If you lose your goggles while in free fall or under canopy, don't blink. If you do, your eyes will freeze shut." I could not believe the sheer beauty beneath. "Incredible. Stupendous," I thought to myself. Bill had suggested that we open our parachutes high up, to take in the scenery for as long as possible on the way down. I opened my parachute at 6,000 feet. I pulled on my left toggle to turn my body to the left and get a view in that direction, then pulled my right toggle to do the same in the other direction. There are no words to describe what I saw or felt as I went down. The North Pole is incredibly beautiful. The air temperature was cold, −50°F, and the air was pristine. There was 0% humidity; the air was cleaner and drier at the North Pole than the air in the Arizona desert, which allowed for a field of vision of 500 miles in all directions. Not one iota of pollution spoiled this northernmost part of our planet Earth.

Another interesting fact about the North Pole is that time does not really exist. The lines of longitude that connect the North and South Poles determine the world's distinct time zones. And, since the lines all converge at the poles, you could say that both poles are in all time zones at the same time. Step one hundred feet in one direction (south), and you're in one time zone; step another hundred feet in a different direction, and you're in a different time zone.

Everywhere I looked, I saw ice. The ice appeared to be different shades of blue, which I learned indicates the age of the ice. The darker the blue, the older the ice. Some of the ice is as hard as granite and, I'm told, believed to be 100,000 years old.

Then I saw the crack in the ice—it was huge. A quick check of my altitude indicated I was at 4,300 feet and felt confident the ice near the crack posed no problem. My descent seemed to take a long time, maybe due to the thick air, but I kept plugging along, enjoying the view. I was doing my best to not miss a single moment of the experience. The next altitude check had me at 4,000 feet with the crack just below me. I was still confident I would not fall into any water. To get to the target area, I followed others whom I believed knew the direction of the target, which ended up being about one and one-quarter miles away.

At fifteen feet, I flared, which means I pulled both steering toggles of my chute to slow myself down for the landing. I landed standing up, in a spot I figured was about 100 yards to the left of our landing target. I had intentionally gone off target, as there was a lot of other parachute traffic already aiming to land there and I did not want to get tangled up with anyone. Another jumper, Carol, landed close by. We were so exhilarated and happy, we gave each other a kiss and a hug.

I found my roommate Bill, who had had a canopy collision with another jumper. The other jumper ended up spiraling down and one of his boots was torn off in the process. Luckily, his boot was located after landing. Bill was really shook up from the incident, but calmed down when he learned the other jumper was not hurt. Another man (also named Bill) had dislocated his right shoulder upon jumping out of the plane into the jet wash. As a result, he did not enjoy the longer free fall most of us did, as he opened his canopy at a height of 1,000 feet.

I'd say that, given these two mishaps, combined with the lost-but-found boot and another jumper who had to do a cutaway (deploying the reserve parachute because the first parachute, the main one, didn't open), our jump was a success. More than anything, I was relieved that I and the others had landed safely. I'm certain I can speak for just about everyone else that day to say we were completely awestruck at the experience—the jump, the scenery, the emotion at just being at the North Pole and completing a successful jump there. So few people are ever presented with such an opportunity.

The next emotion I felt after relief was pride. I was proud of myself—of the fact that, here I was, the least experienced jumper of the group, still in recovery mode from my stroke, and I was on an international expedition to the North Pole and jumping alongside world-famous skydivers. That day, we were all equal—we were just normal people looking to enjoy the experience of a lifetime. For me, it was a very successful jump #87. At one point, I managed to remove my gloves and my hood just long enough for one of my fellow jumpers to take a picture of me next to a U.S. flag that had been erected for this occasion. I had, at Bill Booth's suggestion, brought a small bottle of champagne with me to toast my accomplishment. The bottle was tucked snug inside my jacket and close to my body, to keep it from freezing. Well, the champagne froze anyway, so toasting was not possible.

After our three hours on the pole, the transport helicopter prepared to take groups of twenty-five at a time back to the ice airport. We were one hundred miles from the ice airport, so those of us who remained behind had to wait nearly two hours for the helicopter to return. By the time I was picked up, I had been on the pole twenty-four hours. As I was among the first to land and the last to leave, I really got my money's worth.

Back at the ice airport, the An-74 jet was preparing to take half of the group back to Khatanga. When the jet took off, the weather was beautiful. By the time the jet returned for the rest of the group, the weather had turned ugly and there was virtually no visibility. The pilot was unable to locate the plowed runway of the ice airport and had to make twelve passes. He was only able to land after a flare was sent up. I admit, that was a little scary. What most people don't know is that, at the North Pole, the sun rises on the first day of spring and sets again on the first day of autumn. That means there are six straight months of daylight. The first two weeks of spring are about the only time of year when it's possible to have an ice airport with ice thick enough for a jet or helicopter to land. After that, the ice melts and no aircraft can land there. But, even though the sun is up, the weather can still turn bad, which is exactly what happened on our return trip from the pole. I was glad I had spent the money on the special jump suit Bill had recommended. I credit that suit to keeping me sufficiently warm, comfortable, and protected the entire time, unlike others who were not appropriately dressed for the many hours we spent in the frigid temperatures and who later paid the price. The cold at the North Pole is much more than just a feeling of discomfort—the extreme temperatures can be deadly. Dressing appropriately and being prepared can mean the difference between life and death. I have worn my specialty jump suit only once. I don't expect to ever wear it again, but that was probably the best thousand-dollar investment I've ever made.

Miscellaneous Observations About My North Pole Trip

I saw a lot on my trip to the North Pole, and learned much. Bill Booth did an excellent job as our trip organizer, and he imparted wisdom and expertise that comes only from having made the trip himself. I am forever appreciative and grateful that I had the opportunity to make the journey and was able to take full advantage of it. I would like to be able to say that everything went as planned, but of course it did not. As I mentioned earlier, some mishap or misfortune could have occurred at any step of the way. A few observations I made during my travels could, I suppose, be characterized as mishaps or misfortunes, or as having the potential to cause a mishap.

For example, for the flight from Moscow to Khatanga in Siberia, even though we flew on a commercial jet, we were each responsible for loading our own luggage onto the aircraft. This flight was not like a commercial flight where they take care of your every need.

I also noticed that this plane had bald tires—a condition that jeopardized any kind of safe landing. At one point on the journey, we stopped at a military installation somewhere in Siberia to refuel. We were under strict orders to not disembark the aircraft while, nearby, we saw a Jeep-like vehicle filled with soldiers who were pointing machine guns the entire time at the people who were refueling.

Between the passenger count and all our gear, the plane was overloaded. Inside, two men had to stand on either side of the plane behind where the wings were located to make sure our weight was evenly distributed. I distinctly remember how we all cheered when the plane took off. It needed the entire runway, and even then we weren't sure the plane would be able to lift off the ground.

On the flight to the North Pole, I was wearing a hydration pack that was attached to my body by a harness. The pack was filled with purified water, and I took sips as necessary through an insulated drinking tube, trying to make the water last the entire time I was at the pole. But, as I spent so much time there (remember, I was first on, last off) and was excessively thirsty, I drank all the water. Back in Khatanga, when we were waiting to board the jet to return to Moscow, we encountered a hurry-up-and-wait situation with one delay after another. I was so thirsty, I couldn't wait any longer to get a drink. I had a small drink of tap water, but that small drink did me in. By the time we returned to Moscow, I was sick. At least I had heeded Bill's recommendation to pack Imodium AD. Between my nerves and excitement at each new experience during our ten-day trip and then getting sick from the tap water, when all was said and done, I had lost thirty pounds. What added to my misery was the fact that I had been awake for virtually four days straight—from Easter Sunday, when we left Moscow, to the following Thursday, when we departed Moscow for home.

Another interesting experience I had occurred at the Moscow airport on the return trip. While in Moscow, I had purchased an authentic Russian World War II medal from a street vendor. The medal was about the size of a quarter, and I had packed it in my suitcase. The x-ray machine at the airport detected the medal and, when the guards saw it, they signaled for me to step aside. They opened my suitcase and pulled out the medal. They held it up to my face and said over and over again, "Impossible! Impossible!" That was the only English word these guards knew, and I took them to be saying that it was impossible for me to leave the country with this medal in my possession. They confiscated the medal and detained me away from the rest of my group. I was scared I was going to be locked up. After a time, however, they released me and let me return to my group who was, by then, boarding the plane. Interestingly, they indicated they would mail the medal to me within thirty days, but they never did. Even more interesting, shortly after that experience, I saw the exact same medal for sale in a catalogue, and bought two. "Impossible?" Hardly!

Lastly, I was curious to know the total distance of the trip, and so I calculated the miles for each leg of the journey. From home in Lebanon, Pennsylvania, to New York City was 150 miles. From

New York City to Moscow was 4,664 miles. From Moscow to Khatanga was 2,118 miles. And from Khatanga to the North Pole, another 1,200 miles. I had traveled 8,132 miles to make a single parachute jump! And what an awesome jump it was.

Good Friday Was Especially Good to Me

I've already told you about the Good Friday Last Supper event I envisioned while having dinner with eleven other parachutists and trip organizer Bill Booth the day before leaving on the North Pole skydiving expedition. Even though our dinner did not occur on Good Friday, at two days away at the time, it was close enough and reminded me of the holiness of the day and the value of being spiritual. Since then, two other Good Friday events have occurred that reiterate those sentiments.

I knew I was an experienced jumper, but had always been concerned about my ability to follow steps in proper sequence for safety and, if it came down to it, saving my own life. In the back of my mind, I was always nagged about how the aftereffects of my stroke would affect my ability to take potentially life-saving actions while parachuting. Here I was, the guy who was incapable of following two instructions of first putting a pencil in a box and then a pen. One such life-saving situation while skydiving would be properly handling a cutaway. In parachuting, a cutaway refers to deploying a reserve parachute when the first parachute, the main one, doesn't open. A jumper who finds him- or herself in a situation of having to do a cutaway is going to be under extreme pressure, extreme adrenalin. Would I really be able to do a proper cutaway under such stressful circumstances? I found out on April 2, 1999—Good Friday—on jump number 1,187.

That morning, three of us had gathered at Chambersburg Airport to do a few jumps. The drop zone had a new owner, and this was the first day of operations under that owner. Our jump would be the first of the day, and one of the two other jumpers was the new owner. The plan was the usual: jump at 10,500 feet. But at 2,000 feet, the pilot made the decision that we would not go any higher because there was a lot of cloud cover. That meant we were to jump at an altitude of 2,000 feet. Under normal circumstances, a jumper wants to be under a functioning main parachute by that 2,000-foot altitude, which is easy to do when jumping from the usual 10,000-foot altitude. We were not deterred. We just knew we'd have to act more quickly than usual to get our parachutes open.

As soon as I jumped, I opened my main parachute, but immediately realized I was in what's called a bag-lock situation. A bag lock happens when the parachute deploys but doesn't go out of its bag. I shook the lines twice to try to clear the way for the parachute to open, but nothing worked. By now, I was at 1,000 feet and dropping fast. My life was on the line.

Every parachute has two handles: one on the right to pull when a cutaway is necessary so the main parachute—the one that is not opening—can be completely detached, and one on the left, which is to open the reserve parachute. I pulled both handles at the same time, a move that is not recommended because of the possibility that cords and canopies get tangled up. A proper cutaway should release the main parachute entirely. When doing a cutaway, a jumper should sweep across his or her chest to confirm the main parachute is completely gone. That's the correct way to know the reserve parachute can be opened properly and not get tangled in anything.

I didn't feel panicked, but I was on extreme adrenalin and by then experiencing tunnel vision. Boy, was I in trouble. Normally, I would drop at 120 miles per hour. In a bag lock situation, before the reserve parachute opens, a jumper is dropping almost straight down and with much less resistance, both of which combine to increase drop speed. I was down to an altitude of 200 feet before my reserve parachute opened up. I was literally one second away from hitting the ground, but both amazed and happy to have landed safely. Thankfully, my first cutaway had been a success.

At the time, I wasn't bothered by the experience. Later that night, I told Jane what had happened. I went to bed, closed my eyes, and soon realized that I could have died that day. It took a while, but it's fair to say I was temporarily traumatized by the event. The flip side was realizing I really *did* know how to do the right thing, how to react and respond appropriately in a high-stress situation, in spite of my stroke. The most experienced jumpers say that you need to get back on the horse and jump again right away; otherwise, you might be too scared to ever jump again. I heeded that advice, of course.

In Between the Good Fridays

In between the Good Friday events, something else happened to me that, by most people's standards, was another stroke of bad luck. In August 2002, I was attending a skydiving freefall convention in the village of Rantoul, Illinois. Freefall conventions had always been major events with thousands in attendance and all sorts of jump planes being used—helicopters, biplanes, you name it. That day, I had done six jumps, and was feeling pretty tired from all that activity.

That evening, I was hanging out with a crowd of people, just enjoying the gathering and probably a beer or two. I was sitting on the bed of my pickup truck talking to Jane on my cell phone. She had decided long ago that these events were not for her and was back home in Pennsylvania. She had invited her grandson and his friend for a sleepover. As Jane and I chatted, I was watching a few of the men who were fooling around and setting off fireworks. They started with Roman candles which, if you're not aware, shoot off a series of balls, or exploding shells, that contain all sorts of special fireworks effects like colorful flaming stars and whistles. I should add that Roman candles are illegal in some countries and even in some states because of the danger they pose. (Illinois is not one of those states where it is illegal to possess or shoot off Roman candles.) As my luck would have it, one of the Roman candles fell over and sprayed its contents. A chunk of the firework went directly into my right eye. Needless to say, in my pain, I dropped the phone and everyone in the vicinity was scrambling to get me medical attention. Jane knew something had happened but had no idea what. I can only imagine what she went through as she waited for word. Ten minutes later, she received a call from the wife of one of the friends who was with me at the convention. She explained to Jane what had happened, and, without delay, Jane called her daughter to pick up the boys and made a plane reservation for the following morning.

I was taken to Carle Foundation Hospital in nearby Champaign, where I remained for several days. In the emergency room, I told the doctor, "Give me the straight scoop." The doctor did not mince words. "You're going to be blind in one eye." I was not surprised to hear that. The next day, the doctor performed surgery in an attempt to save the eye for the sake of my appearance, even though I would not be able to see out of it. The outcome of that surgery was not pretty. I felt—and probably looked—more like Frankenstein than my usual "handsome" self.

Back at home, I suffered from intense headaches and sensitivity to light. Jane and I had plans to travel to Austria the following month and I was concerned about how I would be able to travel. Before the trip, I remember one night I was home watching Monday Night Football, sitting in complete darkness, and even then I felt the room was too bright. An eye patch was no help either. After a while, I discovered that standing under a hot shower relieved some of the pain I was feeling. For whatever reason, the hot water running over my head gave me relief. But the minute I turned off the water, the pain returned. Jane and I made our trip, and I dealt with the headaches and light sensitivity as best I could. Jane, for her part, found herself unscrewing lightbulbs here and there throughout Austria to darken things up for me.

Shortly after returning from Austria, I had an appointment with a doctor at Hershey Medical Center. I asked, "Doc, if this was your eye, what would you do?" The doctor said, "I'd have it removed and use a false eye." He explained that the brain works in amazing ways and that the good eye would eventually feel sympathetic pain similar to what was going on with the damaged eye. I didn't have to think twice. "Sign me up."

As routine, the doctor had to check my left eye—the supposed good one—before permanently removing the bad eye. Well, in another stroke of luck (Good? Bad? Your choice), the doctor found a cancerous growth on the white of my left eye. He said, "Bob, you have no choice. The growth has to be removed, but the good news is—" I interrupted him to say, "There's good news?" I was incredulous. I want to think the doctor was empathetic to my cause because he said, "Yes. If you want, we can take care of this right here, right now." And that's exactly what he did. He numbed the eye and cut the growth out.

Once I had recovered from the tumor excision procedure, the same doctor performed surgery to remove my damaged right eye. The relief I felt from the headaches and light sensitivity was immediate. Losing an eye is no fun. But, eliminating that pain only to then lose my life to cancer would have been even less fun. I received the artificial eye and returned to life as usual.

The following August, I attended the annual freefall convention in Illinois again. The first morning, I was on a C-130 high-speed pass cargo jet, flying at about 250 miles per hour. I jumped out of the plane and, wouldn't you know it? My beautiful new prosthetic eye flew out. I did not even realize that had happened. When I landed, someone asked me if I'd lost my eye. After getting over my surprise, I said, "Maybe it's in my goggles." When I checked the goggles, I found nothing. The United States Army Parachute Team, known as the Golden Knights, got word of my loss and volunteered to help search for the eye. One of the men asked me what color the eye was. I said, "I'll take any color you find." We never did find the eye.

Two postscripts to the story about losing my eye: First, Jane and I had traveled to San Francisco and were in a restaurant where I was pouring a bottle of beer into a glass—or so I thought. My depth perception was gone and I was actually pouring the beer alongside the glass and onto the table. What could I do but laugh? In any case, given this lack of depth perception, I was afraid to jump and thought I might have to give up skydiving altogether.

The second postscript is about the person who had set off the fireworks that caused me to lose an eye. He was devastated at what had occurred. To this day, however, we remain friends and see each other about three times a year. I was unable to jump for six weeks, and when I returned to my local drop zone, my friends announced they had taken up a collection for me. I was touched at first, but imagine my surprise when they presented me with a glass jar full of fake rubber and plastic eyeballs! All I could do was shake my head and smile.

Good Friday Episode #3

About a year after the 1999 Good Friday event during which my main parachute failed to open properly, I bought a full-face helmet to wear occasionally while skydiving. I had the helmet specially airbrushed with two very distinct images: a cross and the Grim Reaper. The cross was to signify Good Friday and the Grim Reaper was to commemorate my near-death experience of the previous Good Friday. I called it my lucky helmet.

Fast forward to Good Friday, 2018. Jane and I were in Zephyrhills, Florida, and I was out skydiving, as usual. One of the jumps was a ten-way, which meant ten jumpers were connected for a while as we dropped. I had on my lucky helmet—after all, it was Good Friday. The chin strap was a bit loose, but I didn't give it a second thought, as I had been wearing the helmet that way for a while. At an altitude of about 11,000 feet, I was in the ten-way formation and things were going great. Then, the helmet started vibrating on my head and I knew I was in trouble. And, just like that, the helmet flew off and my prosthetic eye flew out along with it. I knew I would never be able to recover either the helmet or the eye, as they had dropped in an area populated by snakes and alligators and our jump plan did not include jumping into swampland.

That Good Friday, my wallet took a hit at losing both a prosthetic eye that originally cost me $1,300 and a specialty helmet that cost me $1,000. Turns out my "lucky" helmet wasn't so lucky after all.

Interesting (Curious?) Stuff About Bob

Parachuting statistics and achievements:

- I have jumped in 17 different states and 4 different countries.
- Since my first cutaway in 1999, I have had 7 others.
- I have accumulated more than 83 hours of total freefall time. To put that in perspective, from a 10,000-foot jump, the average person is in freefall for 45 seconds before opening the parachute.
- I am a member of POPS, *Parachutists Over Phorty Society*, and smaller groups under POPS: SOS, *Skydivers Over Sixty*; and now JOS, *Jumpers Over Seventy*. I look forward to eventually joining JOES, *Jumpers Over Eighty Society*.
- I have participated in jumps that set multiple state, U.S., and world skydiving records.
- The parachute I use today (Velocity 84) is approximately one-third the size of the parachute I used when I jumped at the North Pole (Manta 288). The numbers represent the square footage of the parachute overhead. The smaller the parachute, the faster the speed on landing. Today I drop at approximately 80 miles per hour and flare at a much higher altitude to reduce some of the landing speed.
- In 1998, I jumped 423 times. Since turning 70 three years ago, I slowed down to 100 or fewer jumps per year.

- I attended the World POPS meet in Chilliwack, British Columbia, in 1999. Because the meet was for parachutists over age 40, one event included rocking chairs, to signify the event was for "older" jumpers. Each jumper was supposed to land on a target of "peas" (small stones), remove his or her parachute, run to the center of the target (if they missed it on landing), and lastly, run to a rocking chair and have a seat. I did not set a record here, as the winner completed the tasks in three seconds, but I sure had fun trying.
- I attended a boogie in Rocky Point, Mexico, at the Sea of Cortez, where I did my first beach landing.
- I made several parachute jumps in the town of Grand Case on the island of St. Martin. One jump was from 10,000 feet and gave full visibility of the entire island.
- Along with six other jumpers, I completed a raft jump from a CASA 212 aircraft.
- I organized record-setting SOS (3) and JOS (1) jumps in Pennsylvania. This involved locating jumpers of the right age who were capable of completing the jump, arranging the plane and the meeting at the drop zone, making sure the jump was held for at least three seconds, and ensuring the jump was fully documented on camera.
- I have participated in 20 record-setting jumps total. One, in particular, was with the POPS and took place in East Stroudsburg, Pennsylvania. We successfully completed a 34-way jump.

Parachuting recognitions:

- Received certificates for completing HALO (high altitude, low opening) jumps, which are most typically done by military personnel.
- Set a world record: As a group of parachutists over age 70, completed a 4-way, 13-point jump.
- Pie in the face: To recognize every 1,000 jumps a parachutist completes, local jumpers "reward" the parachutist with a pie in the face. Though I have nearly 5,500 jumps under my belt, I have only been recognized with a pie in the face twice: in September 1998 when I completed my first 1,000 jumps, and in June 2001, when I completed my $2,000^{th}$ jump. After losing my eye, the gang I jump with didn't feel right about socking me in the face with any more pies. No one wants to be responsible for me losing my remaining good eye!
- When I turned 60, I realized there were no skydiving records set by SOS (Skydivers Over Sixty) in Pennsylvania, so I organized a 9-way jump which we completed successfully on the first attempt. I went on to set other SOS records in Pennsylvania.
- May 5, 2007: I participated in a parachuting tribute to the memory of the 33 people killed in the April 2007 shooting at Virginia Tech. The parachutists formed the letters *VT*. A photo of this jump appeared in the June 2007 issue of *Parachutist* magazine.

- With 59 others from the SOS group, we attempted, unsuccessfully, to set a world record by completing a 60-way jump. The jump took place in Elsinore, California.

- When I turned 70, I knew there were no skydiving records set by JOS (Jumpers Over Seventy) in Pennsylvania. I organized a 5-way jump that had to be completed with the use of two Cessna 182 planes. (The 182 holds only four passengers.) I have since set other JOS skydiving records in Pennsylvania.

- My skydiving career has been prolific and, without listing them all, suffice it to say I have received numerous certificates and recognitions for my skydiving achievements.

I have parachuted from a variety of different aircraft:

- CASA 212
- Hot air balloon
- Short SC-7 Skyvan
- Cessna Grand Caravan
- Cessna Caribou Caravan
- Cessna 182, 206
- Jets: 727, DC-9, IL-76
- Helicopter
- Inverted Pitts Special stunt plane
- Twin Otter
- Ford Tri-Motor
- King Air
- PAC P-750
- C-130 Hercules
- Russian biplane
- Douglas DC-3
- Pilatus Porter
- Glider
- Consolidated B-24
- Lockheed Constellation
- Lockheed P-38 trainer

In August 1999, I parachuted from a B-17 Flying Fortress, the Nine-0-Nine, jumping out the bomb bay door. Sadly, this plane crashed in October 2019 while participating in the "Wings of Freedom" vintage aircraft show at Bradley International Airport in Connecticut.

Also of interest:
- I still take flowers to Sis's grave for her birthday and on holidays and other meaningful occasions.
- I occasionally have breakfast with Sis's brother.
- Every September, since before the Bethlehem Steel plant closed in 1985, I've been attending an annual picnic with other employees. We always had a good time, so I subsequently organized a monthly breakfast with these same former coworkers. To this day, we meet every month for good food and good conversation.
- I've done five New Year's Day polar bear plunges: four locally, in Millards Quarry Pond, in Lebanon County; and one in the Arctic Ocean while on an Alaskan cruise.
- Jane gave me a gift certificate for ten scuba diving lessons. I completed all the lessons and became a certified scuba diver. As much as I enjoyed scuba diving, my ears were bothered by the water pressure and I decided I preferred skydiving to scuba diving.
- In 2008, Jane indulged my "need for speed" by giving me a gift certificate to Doug Foley's Drag Racing School at Maple Grove

Raceway. The certificate entitled me to learn about a dragster and how to drive one, and also to make three runs, which I did. Each run was longer than the preceding one, in terms of distance I drove. I reached 122 miles per hour and was able to "floor it." What an eye-opening experience! I had to laugh when I recalled the DeSoto I took to Maple Grove in 1963 to drag race against an actual competitor. Though the cars have changed, the thrill has not.

- I have driven all different types of vehicles: cars, dragsters, an RV, and a motorcycle. We sold the RV and I eventually gave up the motorcycle.

Supporting others:

- In 2012, I started a fund in support of a longtime friend and fellow skydiver Randy Schroeder who, after surgery, became a paraplegic. Randy needed a wheelchair-accessible van. I set a goal of $50,000 and, though donations fell short, the amount collected gave Randy enough to make a down payment on the vehicle he so badly needed. Today Randy is fully independent and able to move about the country as he needs to. Even though he can no longer parachute, he remains active in the United States Parachute Association and other skydiving groups.
- In 1993, in honor of Sis, I established the Janice E. Atkins Memorial Endowed Scholarship for medical students who met

eligibility requirements. An applicant must be attending Penn State College of Medicine and affiliated with Penn State Milton S. Hershey Medical Center as an intern. Additionally, the student must be living with some sort of physical impairment or handicap, such as being wheelchair-bound or hard of hearing. To date, the scholarship has helped one student every year with the exception of one student, who received the scholarship two years in a row. These deserving students have all gone on to complete their medical training and become practicing physicians.

Optimistic Bob

To date, not much has stopped me from pursuing what I want out of life. Not a quadriplegic wife. Not a seizure. Not a stroke. Not being a widower. Not losing an eye. I simply love life too much to let situations over which I have no control dictate what I can and cannot do. As a naturally curious and interested person, if I see something I want or if something catches my attention, I go after it. Rather than be miserable and complain about everything I *can't* do, I'm a much happier person by figuring out what I love to do and making those things happen. This joie de vivre and enthusiasm is infectious. People love being around others who love life and want to have fun and laugh. And if you haven't noticed, optimism begets hope and more optimism.

I am so glad I took the sage advice of getting back on the horse immediately after my near fatal jump in 1999.

In July 2019, I celebrated the twenty-fifth anniversary of the date of my first parachute jump. In those twenty-five years, I completed 5,475 jumps and have many more jumps ahead of me.

I'm no superhero who walks around patting myself on the back for everything I've accomplished. I don't brag about how I have endured the hardships that have befallen me. To the contrary, I have taken everything in stride and continue to do so even today, with my occasional stuttering and memory loss.

As a recovering stroke victim, I've been fortunate to be able to continue participating in experiences that put my physical and mental capabilities to the test: learning new things, experiencing speed in both the air and on land, discovering new adventures, and traveling across the country or around the globe. I did not develop these interests post-stroke; they have always been a part of my makeup and nature. For that reason, I don't let my speech or memory problems or the fact that I have just one good eye get in the way of what I want to do in life.

Every person is different and strokes affect people differently. I realize that not everyone reading my story will have the same luck I've had in terms of being able to pursue the same level of mental or physical activity. Even if you are unable to continue doing everything you used to do before having a stroke or becoming incapacitated in one form or another, do you not have a different passion, something else you have always wanted to learn or do, an activity you really love?

I am always reminded—and in awe of—people who have lost use of their arms yet manage to paint beautiful artwork using other functioning parts of their body. Or people who report to work every day in a wheelchair. Even Sis, who was completely paralyzed, managed to maintain an upbeat spirit. The list goes on, and the options are endless. As trite as it sounds, there is definitely truth to the saying, "When one door closes, another one opens." It's a matter of opening the right door for you, doing the best you can, and never giving up. Don't aim for perfection—few people ever achieve it. Instead, make your goal simply looking forward to getting out of bed each morning and having fun one day at a time.

I admit I am proud of myself for completing the journey to the North Pole and for becoming an accomplished skydiver. But otherwise, I'm an ordinary guy living a pretty ordinary life. I go to church every Sunday. I work a part-time job driving cars for Manheim Auto Auctions. Jane and I take care of our home and yard together. She has her hobbies and I have mine, but we really enjoy each other's company and share as much of our lives together as we can. And we have wonderful children, grandchildren, and great grandchildren, and try to be as involved in their lives as often as we can. Regardless of whether you consider my life ordinary or not, from my perspective, it's the best life I could ever wish for.

www.ingramcontent.com/pod-product-compliance
Lightning Source LLC
Chambersburg PA
CBHW071715040426
42446CB00011B/2076